A CHAI

CW00402356

The Scheme and Young People with Special Needs

By James Chambers

Edited by Nicholas Gair

The Duke of Edinburgh's Award
5 Prince of Wales Terrace, Kensington, London W8 5PG

The Award Scheme gratefully acknowledges the assistance of the following in the production of this Guide:

Mr Paul Getty's Estate, Stokenchurch
Britnell Court, Old Peoples' Home, Stokenchurch
Princess Marina Centre, Seer Green, Bucks
Beaumont College, Lancaster
Holmescales Riding Centre, Cumbria
Bendrigg Lodge, Kendall, Cumbria
Lady Verney High School, High Wycombe, Bucks
High Wycombe Buckinghamshire College of Higher Education, High Wycombe
Queen Alexandra College for the Blind, Harborne, Birmingham
National Star Centre for Disabled Youth, Ullenwood, Cheltenham
Jubilee Sailing Trust, Southampton
Jacqualine Parkes, Neuro Hospital, Birmingham
Ebrook New Horizons Centre, Great Barr, Birmingham
Mere Green Centre, Sutton Coldfield
Calthorpe Special School, Birmingham
Churchtown Farm Field Studies Centre, Lanlivery, Cornwall
Mill House School for Handicapped Children, Newton-le-Willows, Merseyside
Uphill Ski Club, Spastic Society, London
Kielder Adventure Centre, Northumberland
Stokenchurch Youth Centre, Bucks

PHOTOGRAPHS BY

Mike Blisset
Roger Dixon
Alan Russell
Mike Cotton
Norman Croucher

First edition July 1988

Typeset, printed and bound in Great Britain by
William Clowes Limited, Beccles and London

Designed by Richard Brown FCSD

Copyright © The Duke of Edinburgh's Award

ISBN 0 905425 03 0

The Award Scheme is not competitive; it is a challenge to the individual to do more, to try harder and to reach out to new horizons. The challenge is the same for all and the Scheme offers such a wide choice of activities that most disabled young people, even those with severe handicaps, find it possible to qualify for Awards with little or no variation in the conditions.

The Award Scheme has been in use in Special Schools since its earliest days and its relevance has been proved by a steady growth in its popularity over the years.

Inevitably there have been problems for those with disabilities, and this book will succeed in its purpose if it provides some of the solutions and some encouragement to make the effort to get started. Every journey of discovery begins with the first step.

CONTENTS

INTRODUCTION

Young people with special needs first took part in the Award Scheme in the year it was founded, 1956. Since then the Scheme has grown in popularity as much with them as with any other participants.

In the first *Award Leaders' Handbook* HRH The Prince Philip gave a definition of the Scheme which still holds good today.

"It is designed as an introduction to leisure time activities, a challenge to the individual to personal achievement."

There is no element of competition. Everyone takes part on equal terms. Young people with special needs earn their Awards in exactly the same way as any other participants. The challenges and achievements are personal.

This Guide is not, therefore, a guide to a separate Award Scheme for a particular group of young people—There is no such scheme.

Nor is it a guide to the ways in which parts of the Scheme's programme can be modified or eliminated in order to bring Awards within the reach of people who might otherwise be unable to achieve them—There are no soft options.

Everyone who earns an Award does so by reaching or surpassing the same set of minimum requirements.

This Guide simply presents the Award Scheme from the point of view of young people with special needs. It is designed to be used in conjunction with *Award Handbook*. It shows that the great variety and flexibility within the Scheme allows most people to take part without any need to vary its conditions. It also describes the system of Authorised Variations, under which, in certain circumstances, participants whose disabilities prevent them from meeting the full physical challenge of an activity can earn a reduction in that challenge by adding another equivalent challenge elsewhere in the same activity.

Above all, however, this is a practical guide. It describes the operation of the Award Scheme for the benefit of young people with special needs. Drawing on a broad spectrum of research and on more than thirty years of experience, it shows how obstacles can be overcome and how these young people can join with others and get the best out of everything that the Scheme has to offer.

PART ONE

AN OUTLINE OF THE SCHEME

The Duke of Edinburgh's Award Scheme is a leisure time programme for young people between the ages of 14 and 25 which encourages responsibility, self-reliance, personal discovery and perseverance.

The Scheme is a programme which anybody can take part in and which everybody can enjoy, flexible enough to meet everyone's enthusiasms and aptitudes whatever their background or culture and no matter how plentiful or limited their resources.

The nature and philosophy of the Award have never been better expressed than in Prince Philip's own words:

"The Award Scheme is not an attempt to preach or impose standards by discipline. It is an opportunity for the discovery by experience of oldest truths in human civilisation. It is a sort of do-it-yourself kit for education in the art of civilised living"

The Scheme

Participants follow their chosen activities, largely in their own time, with guidance from someone knowledgeable in each subject, and when they meet minimum set standards of achievement they qualify for an Award.

There are three levels of Award: *Bronze*, *Silver* and *Gold*. For each of these, participants must complete four separate Sections in which the qualifying standards are variously defined in terms of progress, proficiency or sustained effort.

Each level provides a foundation for the next, and each presents a set of challenges which stretch the participants by setting them new targets and wider horizons.

The Awards

Bronze	Silver	Gold
Minimum age 14.	Minimum age 15.	Minimum age 16.
Can be achieved within a year and must take at least six months.	Can be achieved in between a year and 18 months.	Can be achieved in between 18 months and two years.
The upper age limit for the completion of all Awards is the 25th birthday.		

The Sections

Service

Aim: To encourage participants to serve others and to develop both an awareness of the needs of their local community and a sense of their own responsibility.

In this Section participants train for a service, such as First Aid or Conservation, and where possible provide that service as well.

Expeditions

Aim: To encourage a spirit of adventure and discovery and to teach the importance of working in a team with a common purpose.

In this Section participants plan, train for and then undertake a journey in the countryside or on water for a period of two, three or four days in a progressively more challenging environment.

Skills

Aim: To encourage perseverance and the discovery and development of personal interests or social and practical skills.

In this Section participants choose a hobby, a topic to study or some other leisure activity and are required to show progress and sustained interest over a set period.

Physical Recreation

Aim: To encourage determination and an understanding of the lasting satisfaction that can be derived from meeting a physical challenge.

In this Section participants are required to take part in some form of physical recreation and achieve individual progress.

Residential Project (For the Gold Award only)
Aim: To broaden experience through involvement with others in a residential setting.

In this additional project, Gold Award participants undertake a shared activity over a period of five consecutive days in the company of others who are not their everyday companions.

Room for Everyone

The choice of activities within each Section is so wide that the majority of young people, however disadvantaged, can take part on equal terms with the same chance of gaining an Award.

It is recognised, however, that young people who are blind or profoundly deaf may need to use interpreters at some stages, and that those who are restricted to wheelchairs or crutches may require some variation of the conditions which apply to the able bodied.

Authorised Variations

The principle on which variations can be authorised is simple. Any reduction in physical challenge and effort necessitated by a participant's disability must be compensated for by an additional and equivalent demand in another aspect of the same activity.

The right to do less in one area must be earned by doing more in another. Where, for example, young people are incapable of walking over the full distance of an expedition and are therefore allowed to travel over part of it in a vehicle, they may be required to display a higher standard of other expedition skills and to give greater emphasis and time to the purpose of the expedition.

(The full procedure for obtaining an Authorised Variation is laid out in Appendix I)

Special Needs Defined

This Guide covers the operation of the Scheme for young people with three broad categories of disability: Physical, Sensory and Learning Difficulties. This does not include temporary handicapping conditions, such as a broken leg, nor does it include emotional and behavioural difficulties, delinquency or social deprivation, unless they are also associated with one of the three broad categories.

Physical

A physical disability is an impairment of bodily function, other than temporary, which puts the person concerned at a disadvantage and which in the United Kingdom would entitle a child to special educational provision. When this impairment is such as to prevent a young person from fulfilling one or more conditions of the Award, a variation of the conditions may be authorised.

Sensory

A sensory disability is an impairment of sight or hearing which may necessitate some adaptation of the Award's conditions in order to maintain standards of performance or safety.

For example, there are times when a blind or profoundly deaf participant may need a sighted or hearing companion to act as an interpreter. Since this does not amount to a variation, it requires no more than a written clearance from the participant's *Operating Authority* or the Award's *Regional or Territorial Officer*.

Learning Difficulties

Many youngsters with moderate learning difficulties (MLD) have been found to benefit from The Duke of Edinburgh's Award Scheme. No adaptations or variations of the Award's conditions are permitted to such participants, but they outnumber all other young people with special needs and this Guide offers advice on operating the Scheme for their benefit.

Criteria for Entry

No disability is, in itself, a bar to taking part in the Award Scheme. On their way to gaining Awards, participants have overcome considerable learning difficulties and such serious physical impairments as cystic fibrosis, brittle bones and Friedreich's ataxia.

Nevertheless there are, inevitably, some young people who are so severely disabled that they would be unable to fulfil the conditions of the Award, and the generally accepted criteria for entry are as follows:

Physically participants must be capable of meeting all the challenges without suffering any deterioration in the process.

Mentally they must be capable of making a commitment and understanding the nature of that commitment. They must have a basic ability to communicate and enough self-reliance and self-orientation to go on an expedition. They must be capable of choosing their own activities & must have a will to take part in the Award and not just a willingness to be led through it.

Alternatives

Young people who are not permitted by their doctors to undertake the physical challenges need not be entirely excluded from the Scheme. They can always take part in individual Sections, and if they succeed in fulfilling the requirements, the entries in their *Record Books* will be evidence of their achievement. But it must be made clear to them from the outset that this will not be enough to qualify them for an Award.

In the same way, young people who are unable to fulfil the mental criteria for entry may be able to take part in certain Sections. For those who have no hope of success in any Section, it may be better to allow them to join the Award entrants and take part in their activities, other than the Expeditions Section, without obtaining *Record Books*. Although they will have no tangible evidence of achievement, this will at least give them the chance to benefit from the experience.

In addition, for those whose mental capacity is below the threshold of the Bronze Award, there are simpler schemes, such as the Gateway Award of the National Federation of Gateway Clubs, which is recommended for those with severe learning difficulty (SLD), or a local scheme, the Bridge Award, which is run by The Duke of Edinburgh's Award North East Regional Office. The latter begins at an elementary level, but it has also been used successfully as an introduction to the Bronze Award.

Rewards and Challenges

The sense of achievement which every participant feels on gaining an Award is often intensified in young people with special needs.

Many have few opportunities to develop a sense of their own worth. For them progress in each Section brings increased confidence and much more besides.

The Service Section, for example, is chosen time and again as the one which gives them the greatest satisfaction. Here, often for the first time, young people who have spent their lives having things done for them are given the chance to do things for others.

This is the true value of the Award. It manifests and enhances the qualities that are inherent in every young participant.

The courage and determination of young people with special needs who have overcome seemingly endless difficulties to gain Gold Awards have been an inspiration to all the adults who worked with them and to all the entrants who followed in their footsteps.

But the gaining of a Gold Award is an outstanding achievement for anyone. There are some severely handicapped participants for whom it would be unrealistic to expect more than a Bronze Award, and to gain it they too have to demonstrate an exceptional degree of determination.

In the Scheme as in the rest of life, young people with special needs must face extra challenges. Someone who has poor co-ordination, for example, may take hours to do a job which an able bodied person could do in minutes, or days to learn a skill which could be mastered in hours.

Perhaps, in the final analysis, the Award Scheme is different for young people with special needs.
Most of them have to put more into it.
But then most of them get even more out of it as well.

TWO ROADS TO GOLD
ANDREW GALLAHER

Andrew has learning difficulties and is also physically disabled but overcame this in successfully gaining his Gold Award.

"The amount of effort he put into it was phenomenal," said his instructor, "probably ten times that of the average person because of his handicap."

Andrew took up badminton for his Physical Recreation Section.

For his Service Section he studied the care of the elderly and worked at an old people's home, and for the Skills Section he studied metalwork and made a complete tool kit.

Andrew tires easily and although he was unable to cover the full 50 mile distance of a Gold Foot Expedition, he still managed to cover 10 miles a day in the Lake District for four days and made up for the rest by devoting more time and energy to a study of trees and an examination of possible routes for wheelchairs.

His Residential Project, which took place at Paul Getty's estate at Stokenchurch, involved exploring the estate and submitting an oral report on how it could be adapted for use by the disabled.

TWO ROADS TO GOLD
NICOLETTE CONWAY

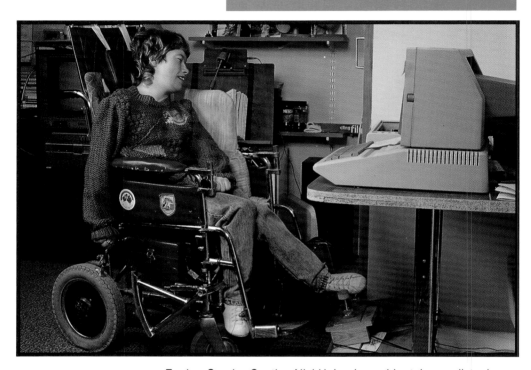

For her Service Section Nicki joined a residents' council, typing nearly all its letters, provided information for a television documentary on how people with handicaps communicate and raised £2,000 on a sponsored mile walk in a special frame, for which she had to train for six months.

For her Physical Recreation Section she studied the origins and history of Yoga and took part in exercises as far as her disability would allow. And for her Skill she took up creative writing, producing three children's stories, three poems, two speeches and a diary of "An Eventful Week".

Her Residential Project took her to Germany, where she studied in a special centre; and her Expedition took her to the Lake

District. She was the only person in her group in a wheelchair, but she still went rock climbing and abseiling with the others— ''The worst bit was going over the top. I had my eyes closed for the first few feet.''

''Nicki has shown that strength of character and perseverance will overcome any physical handicap,'' said her group leader. ''It has been a pleasure to work with such a well motivated and good humoured young lady.''

Nicki is severely disabled by cerebral palsy. She cannot speak, she has no use of her hands, she is confined to a wheelchair and she communicates by operating a word processor with her feet.

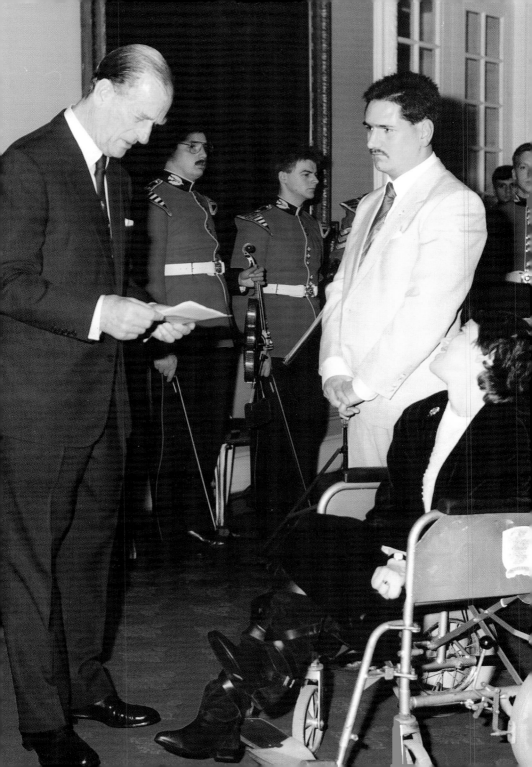

PART TWO
THE SECTIONS

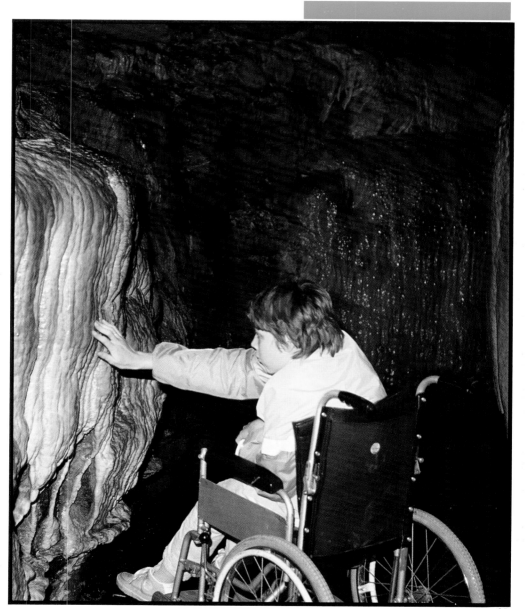

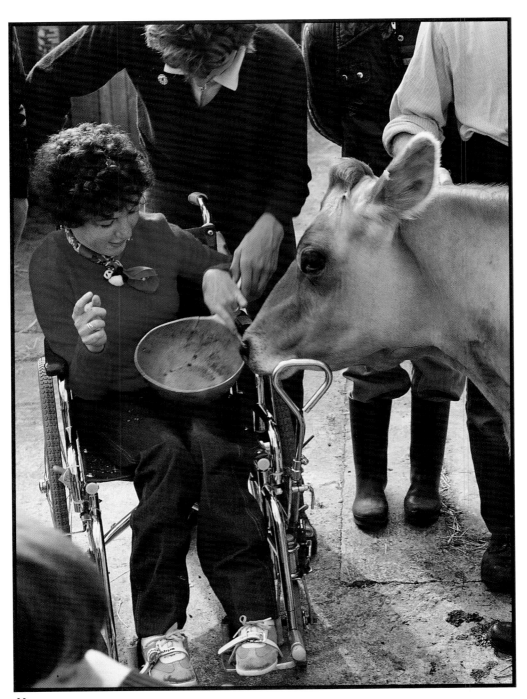

FOR MANY THIS IS THE MOST SIGNIFICANT SECTION. IT GIVES THEM A CHANCE TO HELP OTHERS AND EXERCISE A RESPONSIBILITY WITHIN THE COMMUNITY.

Training

Either: Briefing and counselling sessions leading directly to practical service of a non-specialised nature.

or: Specialised training for later practical service in the field.

Service

There are three categories:

Group 1

Service with a substantial element of practical involvement, e.g. Community Service.

Group 2

Service requiring courses of specialised training, e.g. Care for Animals.

Group 3

Service requiring specific qualifications, e.g. Child Care.

Award Requirements

Bronze	Silver	Gold
Train at a service and/or give practical service to others for 3 months.	Undertake the training and/or give practical service to others for 6 months.	Train and give practical service for at least 12 months.

Details of the required standards for Groups 1 2 and 3 can be found in *Award Handbook*, Chapter 4.

Choosing an Activity

Many young people with special needs can take part in the activities run by the Police and Fire Services, the St. John Ambulance and British Red Cross Society, the hospitals and organisations that help the old, the sick and the disadvantaged. They must be able to satisfy the instructors that they can perform the practical requirements of the service as well as master the theoretical requirements, but if they are spastic, limbless or have other disabilities which would hinder practical work, an oral examination or a taped report will be accepted instead.

For participants with learning difficulties, Group 1 activities are often the most appropriate, since they have a substantial element of practical involvement.

Examples

Wheelchair users have helped to edit a "talking newspaper" for the blind, learned a deaf sign language, served on committees and led games at Gateway Clubs.

In the course of gaining Bronze, Silver and Gold, one spastic young man, who is confined to a wheelchair and has limited use of his hands, passed First Aid and Home Safety examinations orally, chaired a committee, organised two weekend courses for PHAB and acted as treasurer to a workshop where handicapped people made souvenirs. In the course of his various posts he handled a good deal of paperwork and typed a large number of letters with his tongue.

Deaf participants have taken part in a wide variety of Community Services including Life Saving, Child Care and First Aid.

Blind Gold Award holders have worked as volunteers in a geriatric ward and a physiotherapy department.

And slow learners have helped at homes for the disabled and have helped old people with shopping, gardening and decorating.

THIS IS THE SECTION THAT SPURS MANY YOUNG PEOPLE TO JOIN THE AWARD SCHEME—THE ONE THAT APPEALS TO THEIR SENSE OF ADVENTURE.

Each expedition or exploration must have a clearly defined and preconceived purpose, varying from the successful completion of a demanding journey to a more detailed exploration of an area.

For every venture preliminary training in all the following subjects is essential:

Safety Precautions   Use of Compass

Casualty Code   Country Code

Food and Cooking   Camp Craft or Hostelling

Map Reading   Observing and Recording

Award Requirements

Bronze	Silver	Gold
After basic training including one practice journey, carry out a 2-day venture in normal country spending one night away from home and averaging 6 hours per day.	As for Bronze but with 2 practice journeys (1 for Bronze holders), and a 3-day venture in unfamiliar country spending 2 nights away and averaging 7 hours per day.	As for Silver but with 3 practice journeys (1 for Silver holders) and a 4-day venture in wild country including 3 nights away, and averaging 8 hours per day.

Details of required distances for journeys can be found in *Award Handbook*, Chapter 5.

Details of the training required, along with other advice and information is contained in the Award publication *Expedition Guide*.

Choosing an Activity

For Participants with Physical Disabilities the choice between travelling on foot or by bicycle, canoe, rowing boat, sailing dinghy, horse or wheelchair allows a great many to complete an expedition successfully without any need for a variation. Others, however, may need to obtain an Authorised Variation in order to undertake their journey, or part of it, in a motor vehicle.

For Silver and Gold Awards it is possible to choose an exploration which, although it is to be carried out within the context of an expedition, does not specify mileages and permits much of the time required for planned activity to be spent on project work. Nevertheless the conditions still require that a total of at least ten hours should be spent on travelling by personal effort, and here, too, a variation may be authorised.

For the Gold Award participants also have the option of choosing an "Other Adventurous Project", which can depart from the specified conditions provided it has the approval of the participant's *Operating Authority* and the *National Award Office* in advance. (For details see *Award Handbook*, Chapter 5, paragraph 5.)

For Blind Participants the Expedition poses the greatest problems. The best way of learning the practical and imaginative ways of solving these problems is from the schools and youth organisations that have successfully steered participants through the Awards. They can put others in touch with the modern aids and systems which they have used, such as audio compasses, braille maps and models of the routes.

For Deaf Participants the important element to stress is safety. Whistles will not help to find them in a mist, and on an empty road, unlike a city street, they may not expect the car that they cannot hear. They must be well prepared. Those who have partial hearing can keep in touch with radio hearing aids, which can be borrowed from voluntary organisations such as the NCDS.

For Participants with Learning Difficulties this Section imposes considerable intellectual, physical and emotional demands. The organiser must make sure that they understand the concept of an adventurous journey of discovery. A great deal of training is necessary—at least a year in most cases and usually two or even more.

Slow learners need not be able to read an Ordnance Survey map, but they must be able to identify their location on a simpler map and telephone it to base if they need help. One way of achieving this is to start with sketch maps of their school grounds and progress from these through maps of walks, such as those supplied by the Ramblers' Association, to maps with four figure references.

In both training and assessed expeditions, an adult may shadow the group and intervene if safety demands, but if this happens, the group have not passed and must try again.

THIS IS THE SECTION THAT SPANS THE GENERATION GAP—THE ONE THAT GIVES OLDER PEOPLE THE CHANCE TO SHARE THEIR TALENTS AND ENTHUSIASMS. THERE ARE OVER 250 ACTIVITIES TO CHOOSE FROM, INCLUDING PROGRAMMES UNDER HEADINGS SUCH AS APPRECIATION OF THE ARTS, COLLECTIONS, COMMUNICATION, CRAFTS, DRAMA, GARDENING, MUSIC, NATURE, NEEDLECRAFT, PHOTOGRAPHY AND TRANS-PORTATION.

Award Requirements

Follow a hobby, a subject of study or some other leisure interest regularly for a set minimum period improving personal skill or knowledge in the process.

Bronze	Silver	Gold
6 Months	12 Months (6 for those who have completed this Section at Bronze.)	18 Months (12 for those who have completed this Section at Silver.)

If necessary, the choice can be changed once during the set period.

Details of the exact requirements, and programmes available can be found in *Award Handbook* Chapter 6

Choosing an Activity

With its wide choice and its emphasis on perseverance rather than the attainment of set standards, this Section poses no particular problems for young people with special needs.

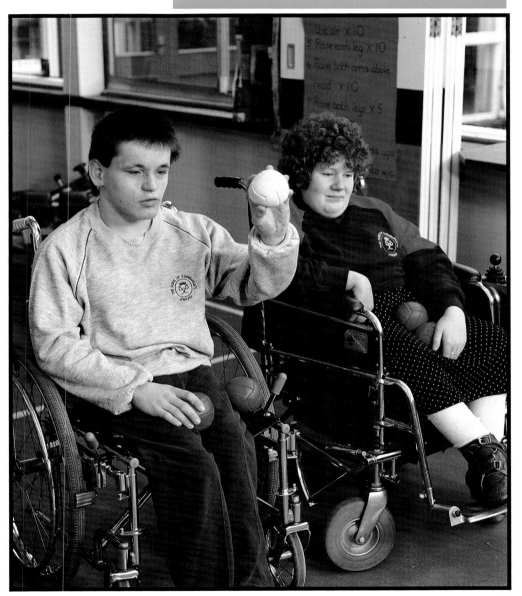

IN THIS SECTION PARTICIPANTS ARE REQUIRED TO TAKE PART IN SOME FORM OF PHYSICAL ACTIVITY AND ACHIEVE INDIVIDUAL PROGRESS. THERE ARE MORE THAN 80 ACTIVITIES TO CHOOSE FROM, NOT ONLY CONVENTIONAL SPORTS AND GAMES BUT ALSO SUCH ACTIVITIES AS DANCING, ROCK CLIMBING, ORIENTEERING AND YOGA.

Activities are divided into Two Groups:

Group 1
Those with measurable or certifiable standards, e.g. Archery, Athletics, Ballet, Fencing, Swimming, Gymnastics.

Group 2
Those for participation only, e.g. Badminton, Bowling, Team Games, Wheelchair Dancing, Wheelchair Marathon.

A scoring system measures achievement in terms of perseverance and improved performance rather than personal prowess.

As a result, the less gifted participants have the same chance to qualify as those who have particular talents.

Points awarded for participation for at least 6 weeks and reaching a given standard or showing improvement are:		
For Bronze 24 points	For Silver 30 points	For Gold 36 points
In all three Awards at least 12 points must be earned for participation (on the basis of 2 for each hourly session with only one session per week counting), the remainder being made up either by continued participation or (in Group 1 only) by the attainment of standards.		

(Full details of the scoring system, including the points awarded for achieving standards in the different activities in Group 1, can be found in *Award Handbook*, Chapter 7.)

Choosing an Activity

Since the scoring system is based on personal performance, young people with special needs can take part in their chosen activities in the same way as other participants and earn their Awards by demonstrating the same degree of determination.

The choice is so wide that there are plenty of activities in which young people with learning difficulties or sensory difficulties can earn the necessary points without any variation in the requirements of the Award.

In the same way, there are many activities in Group 2 (participation only) in which young people with physical disabilities can participate and demonstrate progress.

There are also a number of special schemes in Group 1 activities which young people with physical disabilities can use as Group 2 programmes for earning points for participation.

These include:

Athletics
The following three schemes offer a wide range of events which provide opportunities for those who want to compete with others and take part in Regional or National games. Athletes are classified according to the severity of their impairments.

i The Amateur Athletic Association Five Star Award for physically handicapped children between 12 and 19. This includes the same athletic events as in the BSAD Championships.

ii The Cerebral Palsey International Sports and Recreation Association's track and field events, which include electric wheelchair slalom, bowling, skittles with the aid of a gutter device (Boccia), precision and distance frisbee throwing and other events suitable for young people with severe disabilities.

iii The British Sports Association for the Disabled Senior and Junior Track and Field Championships, which are held regionally and lead to national finals at a major stadium. (BSAD also holds regional and national events in ten other sports, from Archery to Weightlifting).

Gymnastics

The British Amateur Gymnastics Association Awards Scheme is available to all young people including those with special needs.

Swimming

The following schemes are available:

i The Amateur Swimming Association's Encouragement Award Scheme.
ii The Association of Swimming Therapy Proficiency Tests.

Sailing

Special schemes are available from the following organisations:

i The Royal Yachting Association's Seamanship Foundation has a 30ft catamaran which can be chartered for offshore cruising by crews of handicapped and able-bodied sailors, and it helps clubs and other organisations with the provision of specially designed 'Challenger' trimarans which can be sailed single-handed by disabled sailors. The Foundation also runs week long courses in off-shore sailing in conjunction with the Royal National Institute for the Blind.
ii The Jubilee Sailing Trust. The Trust has a sail training ship for disabled/able-bodied cruising.

Riding

The Riding for the Disabled Association Awards.

In some cases young people with physical disabilities can also use these schemes as Group 1 activities and earn points by achieving measurable standards.

For example, the Riding for the Disabled Association's Awards are correlated with the Award Scheme's points system as follows:

Award Points	6	12	18	24
RDA Awards	Grade 3	Grade 4	Grade 5	Grade 6

Where possible, young people with physical disabilities can, of course, take part in Group 1 activities in the usual way. For example, a young man who was paralysed from the waist down was able to achieve the required measurable standards at canoeing.

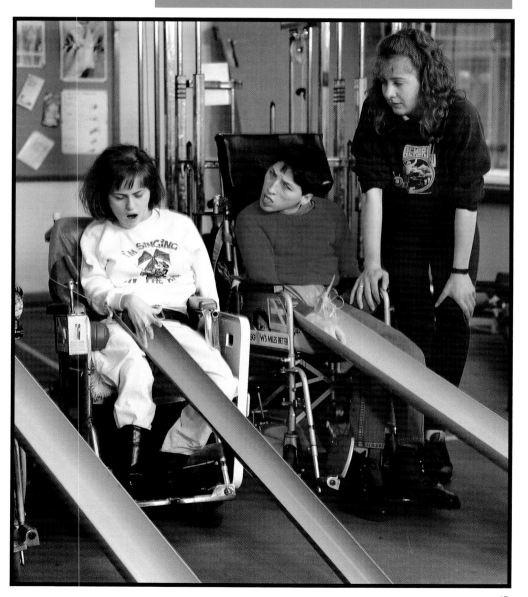

THE DUKE OF
EDINBURGH'S AWARD

SKILLS
PROGRAMMES

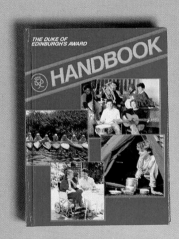

THE DUKE OF EDINBURGH'S AWARD

HANDBOOK

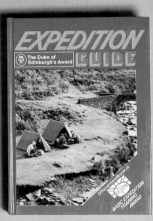

EXPEDITION GUIDE

The Duke of Edinburgh's Award

Official Handbook of
BASIC EXPEDITION
TRAINING
AWARD

THE DUKE OF
EDINBURGH'S
AWARD

THE DUKE OF
EDINBURGH'S
AWARD

INFORMATION AND LITERATURE IS OBTAINABLE NATIONALLY FROM THE AWARD HEAD OFFICE WITH HELP, ADVICE AND SUPPORT BEING AVAILABLE THROUGH THE SCHEME'S TERRITORIAL AND REGIONAL OFFICERS OR LOCAL AWARD COMMITTEES.

Administration

The Scheme is administered in the United Kingdom by a **Head Office** in London, **Territorial Offices** in Scotland, Wales and Northern Ireland and six **Regional Offices** in England.

Operation

Operation of the Scheme is delegated under licence to **Operating Authorities**, who are authorised to grant Awards on behalf of the Duke of Edinburgh and who sponsor the Scheme in any number of **User Units**.

For example, Local Government Authorities are **Operating Authorities** and Schools and youth clubs are **User Units**.

Advisory Panels

At Regional and National level there are also **Handicap Advisory Panels** and within the Awards Head Office the **Assistant Director** is responsible for young people with special needs.

Local Award Committees

These provide a forum for consultation and are composed of representatives from **Operating Authorities**, **User Units** and organisations which provide **Instructors** and **Assessors**, as well as individual helpers.

Their responsibilities include promoting the Scheme and pooling resources.

Field Officers

Field Officers are provided by Local Government Authorities. Their responsibilities include introducing the Scheme in Schools, Youth Groups etc., acting as a contact point for **Leaders** and arranging introductions to **Instructors** etc.

Co-ordinators

Co-ordinators carry out the responsibilities of **Field Officers** within the Voluntary Organisations.

Beyond these, at the heart of the Award Scheme, are the **Instructors** and **Assessors** and the **Leaders** who recruit them and co-ordinate the activities of the participants.

Liaison

It is essential that all **Operating Authorities** and **User Units** keep in close touch with each other through **Regional** or **Territorial Officers**, **Award Committees** etc.

In the first place, this ensures that a standard procedure for helping young people with special needs can be maintained. And secondly, it is the best way of increasing awareness of the Award Scheme and of the growing number of ways in which it can be used jointly by able-bodied and disabled young people.

THE ONLY
ESSENTIAL
QUALITIES FOR
RUNNING A
GROUP ARE
ENTHUSIASM
FOR THE
AWARD
SCHEME, AN
INTEREST IN
WORKING WITH
YOUNG PEOPLE,
PATIENCE AND
PERHAPS A
SENSE OF
HUMOUR .

Most young people with special needs begin taking part in the Award at school. Difficulties often arise therefore when they return to their home area, which can be too far away from the school for them to continue the Award under its guidance. But this can also be a great opportunity. If there is a local Award Group, the desire to continue can be an incentive to go out and make valuable social contact with their own community. If there is no local Award Group, it is only to be hoped that they can persuade a willing adult to start one.

As the Duke of Edinburgh himself has said, the success of the Scheme depends not only on the readiness of young people to respond to its challenges, but also on the thousands of adult helpers who support them.

Getting Started
The first step is simply to learn about the Scheme.

■ Get in touch with your **Regional Officer**, at the address given at the back of this book, who can provide you with a Leader's Pack and any other literature that you may need.

■ Go on one of the Leaders' Courses, which take place over a week-end or on four nights during the week. Details of these are given in the Award's magazine *Award Journal*.

■ And finally, get some practical experience, either helping out generally with an existing Group or organising one of the Sections.

First Build your Team
You cannot begin to assemble your Group until you know that you have access to all the **Instructors**, **Assessors** and other helpers that you will need to make it work. And for a Group that is to contain young people with special needs, this will mean a larger number than would be necessary if they were all able-bodied. Most **Group Leaders** have found that it is best to have a different adult in charge of each Section.

The task is not nearly as difficult as it sounds, however.

Your **Regional Officer** and other contacts within the Award Scheme will be able to introduce you to **Instructors** and to schools and other organisations with a broad experience of running the Scheme for young people with special needs.

As soon as you start you will find that you are surrounded by goodwill and practical support.

Then Build your Group

The best way to interest young people in the Award Scheme is to invite them to a meeting and give them a presentation with one of the Award's promotional films or a slide and tape package which shows it in action.

A guest speaker is also useful, particularly if it is a Gold Award holder who has overcome a disability to gain the Award.

Young people who decide to take part in the Scheme can obtain their *Entrance Packs* from the **Operating Authority**, and as soon as the date of issue has been entered in their *Record Books*, the Award activities can begin.

Remember, however, that each option must be the participant's own choice. And if you need to vary the conditions, avoid the danger of disappointment by having the variation authorised in advance.

Integration not Separation

Whenever possible, set up a mixed group which contains able-bodied young people as well as those with special needs. Experience has shown that this adds a new dimension to the Scheme for everyone.

For example, by joining such a group, young people with special needs who are attending, or have attended, a special school can learn to integrate with an able-bodied community. Hearing participants can choose 'Total Communication' in the Skills Section and act as interpreters for deaf companions at meetings. Sighted participants can experience a deeper awareness of their surroundings on an expedition by undertaking to describe the views in detail to blind companions.

Supporting the Participants

Everyone needs support, and young people who have little self-confidence and low expectations need a great deal more than most.

There will be times when you will have to pitch in with all the support and encouragement you can muster. But if the young people in your Group are to succeed in gaining their Awards, there will also be times when you will have to stand back and resist the temptation to help them.

The key to running a Group for young people with special needs is to be patient and flexible. And the golden rule is to make no assumptions.

Many of these young people have missed out on early childhood experiences such as helping in the house and exploring their environment. As a result they lack the organisational skills and the awareness of their surroundings which enable the rest of us to deal with everyday situations. Simple tasks can be unfamiliar, and this, coupled with a particular disability, can mean that they take much longer than you would expect, even if you are there to support and encourage.

Given the right encouragement, however, there are others who will be able to support you. Many can lighten the burden of their organisers by taking over some of the administration of the Group. It is as wrong to underestimate as to overestimate.

People who have one diminished faculty often develop a surprising capacity in another. Many blind people, for example, have much better memories than sighted people. They don't need to take notes. They can remember telephone numbers and grid references after hearing them only once.

On one expedition, when a map was lost, the blind members of the group led everyone home safely in the dark by retracing their steps and remembering every turn on their route.

Keeping them going

For most adult organisers the main challenge in running a group for any young people is not getting them started but keeping them going. It's up to you to keep up their momentum and morale.

■ Keep their *Record Books* up to date.

■ Hold regular meetings.

■ Encourage them to run their own newsletter.

■ Where it is within their capabilities, encourage them to move on to Silver and Gold as soon as they have gained their Bronze.

■ If you are running a group within a school, make sure that, before they leave, your participants are in touch with an adult or a group who can help them to continue with the Scheme. This is particularly important for young people with sensory disabilities, who may need the support of a hearing or sighted adult at meetings etc.

Parents and Guardians

The parents and guardians of young people with special needs also have a vital role to play, not only in encouraging them but also in more practical ways, such as providing transport.

Whenever possible therefore it is essential to enlist their support from the outset. Point out to them how they can help. Make sure that they understand the nature of the Scheme and that where necessary they are prepared to give their consent. (Some *Operating Authorities* require written consent from the parents or guardians of participants under the age of 18.)

Assessment

Assessors must be suitably qualified and approved by the *Operating Authority*, and they must observe the conditions laid down in *Award Handbook*.

It is sometimes difficult to assess the achievements of young people with special needs. The **Assessors** must be sympathetic and yet at the same time dispassionate. Their most important responsibilities are to ensure that the standards of the Awards are maintained and that they are seen to be even-handed in their assessment of all participants, whether they are able-bodied or not.

Publicity
Award Scheme events are newsworthy and the gaining of an Award deserves to be noticed.

Stories in the media, displays of Award activities and public presentations of Bronze and Silver Awards are among the best ways of attracting new members to your group and encouraging others to carry on and go for Gold.

The essence of good publicity, however, is to show the common standards achieved by everyone, and not to treat young people with special needs as though they were different from other participants.

DETAILED INSTRUCTIONS ON THE PLANNING AND RUNNING OF AN EXPEDITION CAN BE FOUND IN THE *EXPEDITION GUIDE.* WHAT FOLLOWS IS SIMPLY A COLLECTION OF ADDITIONAL TIPS FOR THE RUNNING OF GROUPS WHICH CONTAIN YOUNG PEOPLE WITH SPECIAL NEEDS .

Planning

Plan well ahead. Find out everything you can about the area in which you intend to hold your Expedition. Contact the people associated with the area such as National Park Youth & Schools Liaison Officers etc., tell them what you intend to do and listen to their advice.

Start at a place where you have all the facilities that you may need—lavatories, hire of bicycles etc.

Finish at a place where there is something else of interest to do or see—so that the people who get there first are not just hanging around waiting for other groups to arrive.

Make sure that there are lavatories along your route—not all physically handicapped young people can use the nearest piece of cover.

Check that you have all the equipment that you will need— a tail-lift on your mini-bus if some of your participants are in wheelchairs—and spare parts for the wheelchairs.

Choose a route that is appropriate—make sure that the path is suitable for wheelchairs, for example, or that it does not take young people with poor balance along the edge of a tall cliff.

Pick suitable accommodation for participants who will not be sleeping under canvas. Camping barns are often better for wheelchairs than hostels with narrow doors or no washing facilities on the ground floor.

The Expeditions Section is the one which presents the greatest difficulties for young people with special needs.

It is often the Section which gives them the greatest self-confidence as well. But equally it produces the largest number of challenges for organisers and *Assessors*. Almost every piece of practical advice which can be applied to the running of other sections can also be applied at some time or another to the running of an expedition.

Reconnaissance

No matter how well you have planned, you must check everything. And you can only do that by seeing for yourself.

A route that seems suitable can in fact be beset with obstacles.

Gates can be locked, and if you want to get wheelchairs through them, you will have to know where the keys are.

Some paths which can sometimes be suitable for wheelchairs can also be impassable for them, for example when rain has made the going heavy or when horses have churned up the ground.

Preparation

Remember that training will take much longer for many young people with special needs than it would for the able-bodied.

Use diagrams rather than written instructions for young people with learning difficulties.

Practise everything—even packing and unpacking.

If there are young people in your group who have never been away from home before, practice that as well—spend a couple of nights in your local youth hostel.

Learn everything about the needs of the young people in your group—special diets, drugs etc.

Setting out

Check everything again.

Make sure that everyone has all the clothes that you told them they would need.

Make sure that the clothes fit and that they have worn them before—a painful pair of new shoes can be as useless as the wrong shoes.

Make sure that nobody is carrying any unnecessary tins of chocolate pudding etc.

And finally make sure that they all enjoy themselves and keep your sense of humour when, despite your careful planning, things start to go wrong.

Among many other things, the Award Scheme is meant to be fun.

THE PROCEDURE FOR OBTAINING
AUTHORISED VARIATIONS

Forms

There are two forms which are used by *Operating Authorities* in considering and recording individual cases:

PD/V The Application for a Variation,

PD/M The Medical Questionnaire or Doctor's Form.

Authorisation

The degree of scrutiny increases with each level of the Award:

Bronze

Approval of proposed variations must be given by the *Operating Authority* concerned or its responsible representative in consultation with the doctor who attends the physically handicapped participant. The *Operating Authority* may at its discretion require the *User Unit* to complete forms PD/V and PD/M.

Silver

Approval must be given by the *Operating Authority* concerned or its responsible representative in consultation with:

1. The doctor who attends the participant,

2. Some additional person or persons who have special knowledge or experience in the field of the physically handicapped.

The *Operating Authority* may at its discretion require the *User Unit* to complete forms PD/V and PD/M.

Gold

Approval must be confirmed by the appropriate Award Scheme *Territorial or Regional Officer* in consultation with:

1. The Operating Authority,

2. The doctor who attends the participant,

3. Some additional person or persons who have special knowledge or experience in the field of the physically handicapped.

Forms PD/V and PD/M must always be used. Failure to follow the procedure can result in an Award being witheld.

Specialist advice can be obtained from the **National Handicap Panel** through **Territorial and Regional Officers**, and it is recommended that it should always be sought in cases where there are no know precedents.

National Operating Authorities should make their submissions for variations to the **Assistant Director** at the **London Award Office**.

The forms PD/V & PD/M for application to vary the conditions

CONFIDENTIAL

The Duke of Edinburgh's Award

Variations Form for Physically Handicapped Participants Undertaking the Silver or Gold Award

Name of Participant _____ Date of Birth _____

Operating Authority _____

Reminder

a This form is to be completed if any variation of the conditions is considered necessary for either the Silver or Gold Award. It is *not* normally required in the case of the Bronze Award but Operating Authorities may use it if they find it convenient for their system of assessment and records.

b Before completion, reference should be made to the Award publication *Challenge to the Individual*, The System of Variations.

1. Has he/she already entered for Silver/Gold Award? _____

2. If so, what Sections are being attempted or have been attempted under normal conditions? _____

3. In which Section(s) is variation of the condition desired? (Full details to be given on form attached). _____

4. Additional comments, if any, to support application.
(If more space is required, please write on another sheet).

Signed: _____

Position: _____

Date: _____

N.B. This is a confidential document for consideration by those responsible for approving variations of conditions for the Silver Award (your Operating Authority) or Gold Award (your Territorial or Regional Officer).

Proposed Variations of Conditions

In accordance with the conditions for authorisation in Award publication *Challenge to the Individual.*

Participant's Name _____

Service
(Limitation of Practical Work, if any)

_____
_____

Expeditions

_____
_____

Skills
(Indicate means of overcoming any special difficulties)

_____
_____

Physical Recreation

_____
_____

Variations authorised by:

For Silver Award (Signed) _____ (Operating Authority)

For Gold Award (Signed) _____
Territorial/Regional Officer of _____

Note. If more space is required to describe proposed variations, for example in relation to the Residential Qualification, please use an additional page.

CONFIDENTIAL

The Duke of Edinburgh's Award — Medical Questionnaire for intending participants with physical handicaps

Name of Participant _____ Date of Birth _____

Please fill in answers to the questions as far as they are applicable to the handicapped young person concerned.

1. What is the nature of the participant's disability? _____

2. Diagnosis and date of onset? _____

3. Is the condition still active or progressive? _____

4. Has the participant full use of both hands; if not to what extent is
their use impaired? _____

5. Can the participant:

   a walk unaided or with crutches? _____

   b if so, roughly how far? _____

   c all the time? _____

   d some of the time? _____

6. Does the participant have to wear any appliances, e.g. calipers,
spinal jacket? _____

7. Can he/she walk up and down stairs unaided? _____

8. Can he/she use a hand-propelled or motor chair? _____

9. Does participant require help in looking after him/herself, e.g. with washing and dressing; in bathroom and lavatory?

_____

10. a Is participant subject to fits? Is so, to what extent?

_____

b Does the participant administer his/her own medication?

_____

11. Does he/she suffer from more than one handicap e.g. additional sight, hearing or speech defect?

_____

12. Have you any reservations about the proposed participant taking part in the Award Scheme, or comments not covered by the foregoing questions?

_____

Signed _____

_____ (Medical Adviser)

Address _____

_____ Date _____

N.B. This is a confidential document for consideration by those responsible for approving variations of conditions for the Gold Award. Operating Authorities who wish to use it for participants for the Bronze or Silver Awards may, of course, do so but a simple note from the doctor that he/she has no reservations as to the proposed programme of activities, i.e. does not anticipate them causing a deterioration in the participant's physical condition, is all that is necessary in most cases.

Amateur Athletic Association Five Star Award Scheme
c/o British Sports Association for the Disabled.

Amateur Swimming Association Awards
Harold Fern House, Derby Square, Loughborough, Leicestershire LE11 0AL

Association of Swimming Therapy
4 Oak Street, Shrewsbury, Shropshire SY3 7RH

The Boys' Brigade
Felden Lodge, Felden, Hemel Hempstead, Hertfordshire HP3 0BL

The Bridge Award
c/o The Duke of Edinburgh's Award North East Regional Office, PO Box 2, Hadrian Road, Wallsend, Tyne and Wear NG28 6QZ

British Amateur Gymnastics Association
Head Office: 2 Buckingham Avenue East, Slough, Berkshire SL1 3EA
Technical Department: Ford Hall, Lilleshall National Sports Centre, Nr. Newport, Shropshire TF10 9NB

The British Polio Fellowship
The Bell Close, West End Road, Ryslip, Middlesex HA4 6LP

The British Red Cross Society
9 Grosvenor Crescent, London SW1

British Sports Association for the Disabled
Hayward House, Barnard Crescent, Aylesbury, Bucks
HP21 8PP

The Calvert Trust (Adventure Centre for Disabled
People)
Little Crosthwaite, Keswick, Cumbria CA12 4QD

Central Council for Physical Recreation
Francis House, Francis Street, London SW1P 1DE

**Cerebal Palsy International Sport and Recreation
Association**
Sports Technical Secretary: 2 Grange Road, Edwalton,
Nottingham NG12 4BT

Churchtown Farm Field Studies Centre
(Outdoor Adventure for Disabled People) Lanlivery,
Bodmin, Cornwall

Jubilee Sailing Trust
P.O. Box 180, The Docks, Southampton, Hants SO9 7NF

MENCAP
123 Golden Lane, London EC1

MIND (National Association for Mental Health)
22 Harley Street, London W1

**The Multiple Sclerosis Society of Great Britain
and Northern Ireland**
22 Effie Road, London SW6

The National Association of Youth Clubs
Keswick House, 30 Peacock Lane, Leicester LE1 5NY

National Federation of Gateway Clubs
117 Golden Lane, London EC1Y 0RT

National Youth Bureau
17–23 Albion Street, Leicester LE1 6GD

PHAB
Tavistock House North, Tavistock Square, London
WC1H 9HX

Pony Club
The British Equestrian Centre, Stoneleigh, Warwickshire
CV8 2LR

Riding for the Disabled
Avenue R, National Agricultural Centre, Kenilworth,
Warwickshire CV8 2LY

**Royal Association for Disability and
Rehabilitation**
25 Mortimer Street, London W1N 8AB

The Royal National Institute for the Blind
224 Great Portland Street, London W1

The Royal National Institute for the Deaf
105 Gower Street, London

**The Royal Yachting Association Seamanship
Foundation**
RYA House, Romsey Road, Eastleigh, Hampshire SO5
4YA

Salvation Army
101 Queen Victoria Street, London EC4 4EP

The Scout Association
65 Queensgate, London SW7

The Spastics Society
12 Park Crescent, London

The Sports Council
16 Upper Woburn Place, London W1

St John Ambulance Cadets
1 Grosvenor Crescent, London SW1X 7EF

TOC H
1 Forest Close, Wendover, Aylesbury, Buckinghamshire HP22 6BT

Youth Hostels Association
Trevelyan House, 8 St Stephen's Hill, St Albans, Herts AL1 2DY

NORTHERN IRELAND
A list of useful addresses may be found in the *Directory of Sport and Recreational Opportunities for Disabled People* obtainable from:

Northern Ireland Sports Council
c/o House of Sport, Upper Malone, Belfast.

SCOTLAND
Useful addresses can be obtained from:

Scottish Sports Council
1 St. Colme Street, Edinburgh, EH3 6AA.

WALES
Useful addresses can be obtained from:

Sports Council for Wales
National Sports Centre for Wales, Sophia Gardens, Cardiff, CF1 9FW.

BIBLIOGRAPHY

The Duke of Edinburgh's Award, *Award Handbook*

The Duke of Edinburgh's Award, *Expedition Guide*

The Extension Activities Handbook (A Guide to Scouting with the Handicapped), Scout Bookshops Ltd., Churchill Industrial Estate, Lancing, Sussex.

Outdoor Pursuits for Disabled People, N. E. Croucher.

Out of Doors with Handicapped People, Mike Cotton.

Outdoor Adventure for Handicapped People, Mike Cotton.

Access to Music for the Physically Handicapped School Child and School Leaver, D. J. Kennard; Disabled Living Foundation, 346 Kensington High Street, London W14 8NS.

Special Education Needs: Report of the Committee of Enquiry into the Education of Handicapped Children and Young People, 1978, H. M. Warnock.

Physical Education for the Physically Handicapped, 1976, the Department of Education and Science; The Government Bookshop, Her Majesty's Stationery Office, PO Box 659, London SE1.

Physical Education for Special Needs, Lillian Groves, Ed., Cambridge University Press, 1979.

Guide to Fishing Facilities for Disabled Anglers, National Anglers Council, 5 Cowgate, Peterborough PE1 1LR.

Watersports for the Disabled, Royal Yachting Association, Victoria Way, Woking, Surrey.